These questions are answered by:

____

____

____

All your answers are not wrong
All your answers are not always right
All come from your bright or dark thoughts
All come truly, deeply from your heart and soul
And all come to define who you are at this very moment

DAY 1

What does it mean to live a life of mystery?

DAY 2

What is the one thing that no one seems to have in mind when making plans?

DAY 3

If you'll be given your own 15 minutes of fame, what would you do?

DAY 4

What's your first reaction when you think about someone like your brother/sister?

DAY 5

What do you think will be a positive outcome of the conversation?

DAY 6

List of things that have been banned

If you could be an extra in any of your favorite movies, which dream movie would you choose?

How can you help your son cope with rejection?

Did you recently have an interesting conversation? What did you talked about?

DAY 10

What is one thing the average person can do today to achieve maximum happiness?

DAY 11

What's your most important personal gift?

DAY 12

What is one thing you have in common with all your groups?

DAY 13

Will you be willing to sacrifice time and energy to find out the truth?

DAY 14

Explain outdoor living to a person with an apartment in the city.

DAY 15

If you had to choose one thing that you believe should be banned and the other thing that should remain legal, what would you choose and why?

DAY 16

How do you deal with the feeling that the people around you will never tell you the truth and you will have to rely on yourself?

DAY 17

What is your most invaluable possession and why?

DAY 18

Say something about a girl's face

DAY 19

How do you deal with someone who is just not that kind of a person?

DAY 20

If you were the principal of this school, what would you do?

DAY 21

Do you have confidence in yourself or others? Why?

DAY 22

Say something about your family that will get them excited.

DAY 23

What is the one thing you have that everyone else wants?

DAY 24

What if you are nothing except your identity?

DAY 25

What do you dislike most about your appearance?

DAY 26

Where do you find the information to make things easier?

DAY 27

Lost in outer-space, she... [continue the sentence]

DAY 28

List of things that can improve your productivity

DAY 29

If you could have any item that would only affect you, what would it be?

DAY 30

What's your superhero name and what powers do you have?

DAY 31

Do you feel angry when you don't do anything? Why?

DAY 32

If you had to decide between having enough money and not wanting to die alone, which would you choose?

DAY 33

Would you rather wear pants or dress up? Why?

DAY 34

If you had to choose, would you prefer to have done it your way or would you have liked to do it the other way and then you had to change it?

DAY 35

What is something that you would like to achieve and why?

DAY 36

How would you describe the feeling of being with someone when you know that the other person is worried about something?

DAY 37

List of things that you have learned

DAY 38

*What would happen if you loved your neighbor as yourself?
What if everyone did?*

DAY 39

What would you do if you lost an idea?

DAY 40

What is one thing that is wrong with your life right now?

DAY 41

When was the last time you were able to find yourself in a bad situation?

DAY 42

Describe your favorite toy, why do you like it best?

DAY 43

Talk about the least favorite part of your body.

DAY 44

What would it take for that to change?

DAY 45

Will you make a wish in the future?

DAY 46

What are some of the big challenges that you faced in your life?

DAY 47

Would you rather sit in a room with ten scientists from the International Space Station or four astronauts from the Curiosity Mars rover?

DAY 48

List of things that make you enjoy eating food

DAY 49

Why are your feelings so bad that you want to die?

DAY 50

What is one thing you have in common with your boss?

DAY 51

Do you prefer to feel in control? Why?

DAY 52

Would you rather make us laugh but also cry and be happy?

DAY 53

What do you think about his/her hobbies?

DAY 54

How are you using your time?

DAY 55

What's your first reaction when you think of a good old fashioned 'taste of the country'?

DAY 56

What's easier done than said?

DAY 57

What is your philosophy of life?

DAY 58

What's your favorite animal?

____

____

____

____

____

DAY 59

What's so horrible about the world that it isn't worth trying to fix?

____

____

____

____

____

DAY 60

List of things that you want to finish

DAY 61

What do you have to lose?

DAY 62

List of things that works for you

DAY 63

How would you respond if someone came to you crying?

DAY 64

How would you describe the feeling of being underwater?

DAY 65

Would you rather have a non-human or a robot?

DAY 66

Do you play a character? If so, who did you pick and why?

What is perfect love?

What do people find most fascinating about you?

How do you deal with the reality of the way you're used to living?

DAY 70

What is the one thing you've learned in your 20-plus years?

DAY 71

If you could be one super beautiful brain, what would you be?

DAY 72

Does that bother you when people are mean? Why?

DAY 73

What would you say about what's going on in the world?

DAY 74

What is your favorite kind of cake?

DAY 75

What is the one thing that you would not tell your 17-year-old self?

DAY 76

Do you have a fear of missing out? Why?

DAY 77

Do you love watching music videos? Which ones are your favorite?

DAY 78

What makes you passionate about your craft?

DAY 79

What's the worst thing about the new rule?

DAY 80

How do you think you would be received in God's sight?

DAY 81

How do you handle friends that want to listen in and take control?

DAY 82

What is one thing you want people to know about your life?

DAY 83

If you could be any race, which would you choose and why?

DAY 84

Think of the best teacher you ever had. Why were they a good teacher?

DAY 85

What do you first remember about you and your mother?

DAY 86

How would you describe the feeling of being at this stage of your life?

DAY 87

What attracted you most to the opposite sex?

DAY 88

In your dreams, where do you dream of going?

DAY 89

When was the last time I actually felt sad?

DAY 90

How do you deal with feelings of loneliness?

DAY 91

How do you deal with the possibility that someone you trust might be lying to you?

DAY 92

Who are your favorite artists?

DAY 93

Why do you do things you shouldn't?

DAY 94

How do you feel when someone's telling you they like you?

DAY 95

Do you know the first time you made you're-going-to-have-to-work-really-hard talk about yourself? When was it?

DAY 96

If you could take another life, which one would it be?

DAY 97

How would you describe the feeling of entering?

DAY 98

So what is your dream?

DAY 99

If you had to pick one single moment that made you a better person, this would be when?

DAY 100

What is your sex-drive?

DAY 101

What's the best thing you've eaten in the last week?

DAY 102

What is the most significant area of improvement in your life?

DAY 103

What songs have you completely memorized?

DAY 104

Will you be the one to take a bow?

DAY 105

Where do you get your news?

DAY 106

What did you do today that made you smile and proud of yourself?

DAY 107

How do you avoid bad days?

DAY 108

Why do you think some people smoke/drink?

DAY 109

What does it mean to be a good father?

DAY 110

What are you talking about?

DAY 111

How would you describe the feeling of seeing the light?

DAY 112

Who are your favorite athletes?

DAY 113

Who do you live for?

DAY 114

When you were a child, how did you imagine your adult life?
How is it similar or different from what you imagined?

DAY 115

What other shows are you watching?

DAY 116

When you're learning a new language, what is the first thing you think about?

DAY 117

What do you enjoy giving people?

DAY 118

What would happen if ghosts were to unite?

DAY 119

Tell about a time when someone made you feel welcomed or accepted? What did they do and how did it make you feel?

DAY 120

How would you describe the feeling of being proud?

DAY 121

Would you rather have a job that is easy and predictable or one that is hard to control, unpredictable, risky and often full of risks?

DAY 122

How do you deal with people who hate you so much?

DAY 123

If you had to choose one thing about the world you are most worried about right now, what would it be?

DAY 124

What do you regret and why?

DAY 125

Who has had a strong influence on your life?

DAY 126

What would you say to people who think they've seen your face but haven't?

DAY 127

What places in your life are places you are scared of?

DAY 128

What was it that got you hooked on reading?

DAY 129

What is your favorite word?

DAY 130

Who are your heroes in this world?

DAY 131

When did you feel you really connected with someone?

DAY 132

What if you're allowed to see what happens to you 10 years from now? Would you like to see it?

DAY 133

How do you got your scars? Tell the story.

DAY 134

Do you prefer to make your meals or have someone cook them for you? Why?

DAY 135

What was it that you loved about it that made you want to do it?

DAY 136

If you could have one question answered, what would it be?

DAY 137

If you could be anything in this world, what would it be and why?

DAY 138

How did you find your true self?

DAY 139

Do you ever feel embarrassed? Why?

DAY 140

What does the word "God" mean to you and why?

DAY 141

How do you deal with someone who wants to be part of the conversation but you just can't because they want you to be present?

How do you deal with a person who is always telling you how bad your day is?

What is the most significant nonconventional force shaping global trends?

If you had to choose one thing in the world to be completely happy in, what would it be?

DAY 145

What's your favorite character?

DAY 146

If you could take a single thing from an event or something that you think was inspirational, what would it be?

DAY 147

What is one thing you have in common with your favorite band?

DAY 148

What is the one thing that would make you happy?

DAY 149

Describe a time when you returned to a place from your past and how you and the place had changed.

DAY 150

What are you listening to right now?

What are your current relationships like?

How do your kids learn about the world in school?

What would the person you're talking to say about the day?

What is the most embarrassing thing you've ever done to yourself?

How do you react when you realize you've made a mistake?

Where you got your name from?

DAY 157

What is the one thing that you regret most about your career?

DAY 158

What 10 things you can do every day if you have $5,000 a day?

DAY 159

Is there anything you would have done differently? What is it?

What is the one thing that you don't think makes a person smart?

What are the top five unanswered questions?

If there was a time when you were feeling down before, what kept you going?

DAY 163

What's your first reaction when you see the new movie?

DAY 164

What is something you do when your mind is not thinking?

DAY 165

What keeps you up at night?

DAY 166

What can you do to give back?

DAY 167

What is most important for you to achieve your dream?

DAY 168

Would you rather eat it all, or save it, or give it to someone?

DAY 169

What parts of nature do you like best?

DAY 170

How would you describe the feeling of being able to understand everything so well?

DAY 171

What is the one thing that bugs you about fast food today?

DAY 172

What is the most important goal you have for the rest of your life?

DAY 173

How would you describe the feeling of being indisposed?

DAY 174

If you could give one piece of advice or a self-belief to every child, what would it be and why?

DAY 175

What can you do to be a better person today?

DAY 176

What is the one thing you've learned that has helped you grow?

DAY 177

Do you consider yourself an introvert or an extrovert? Tell about it.

DAY 178

Where would you like to travel? How would you get there?

DAY 179

What makes you think the other side is not telling the truth?

DAY 180

What's your philosophy in life?

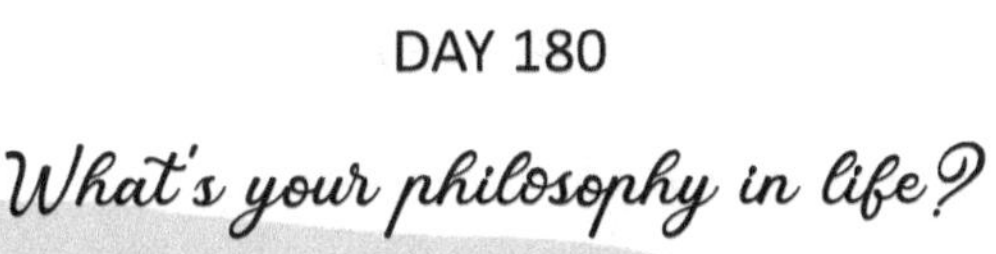

DAY 181

What is your favorite costume?

DAY 182

What are your three most-frequented places at home?

DAY 183

What is the funniest thing someone has ever said to you?

DAY 184

Who has changed you the most and why?

DAY 185

How do you deal with problems that can't be solved?

DAY 186

Where is the most interesting place you've been?

DAY 187

What makes you want to live?

DAY 188

List of things that you might want to create

DAY 189

List of things that make you cringe

DAY 190

What do your parents need?

DAY 191

What would you invent to make life better?

DAY 192

How would you describe the feeling of being robbed?

DAY 193

Write a letter to yourself 10 years in the future.

DAY 194

Name three people whose lives have been improved by knowing
you and explain why.

DAY 195

How do you feel about living on a perpetual budget?

DAY 196

What is an unusual form of transportation you have used?

DAY 197

What do you like to do when you're bored?

DAY 198

*If you had to choose one thing to keep with yourself forever,
what would it be and why?*

DAY 199

What will you achieve in your life today?

DAY 200

What made you go out today and why?

DAY 201

Who would you rather listen to, someone who is smart and knows how to be smart or someone who never stops learning in all their life?

DAY 202

What did your family do on Sundays as a child?

DAY 203

List of things that could be faked

DAY 204

What was the happiest moment in your life?

DAY 205

Say something that'll make it hurt even more.

DAY 206

Would you rather be able to speak or not?

DAY 207

What do you eat when you have a hangover?

If you had to choose one thing to do today in your spare time, what would the top thing be?

List of things that affect sleep

How would you describe the feeling of being captured?

DAY 211

What's something you have to tell everyone but you'll never tell anyone?

DAY 212

Do you ever think "I wish I would have done this or that"? Why? Why not?

DAY 213

If you had to choose between capitalism and socialism, which would you rather have?

DAY 214

List of things that you already found

DAY 215

What are some small things that make your day better?

DAY 216

How would you describe the feeling of being in a relationship with someone that you know isn't a perfect match?

DAY 217

Would you rather spend a week adrift at sea in a life raft or spend one month in the coldest place on earth? Why?

DAY 218

Are you in an abusive relationship? How?

DAY 219

If you had to choose one thing that you want to be remembered for, what would it be?

What do you like to drink for breakfast?

Do you feel you can be happy with your choices? Why?

List of things that are difficult to understand

DAY 223

What is the best advice anyone has ever given you?

DAY 224

Do you see your best friend from the inside out?

DAY 225

If you could only have one item out of your favorite set, which would you choose?

DAY 226

If you weren't a human, what animal would you be?

DAY 227

Why do you think gender differences exist?

DAY 228

What would you do differently now and why?

DAY 229

Say something that isn't a lie.

DAY 230

*If you had to choose one thing that most defines the genre,
what would it be?*

DAY 231

*How do you deal with someone who says "I don't know? I'm
not sure"? How do you get the point across?*

DAY 232

Do you believe that you have to utter a wish every 11:11 PM? Why?

DAY 233

What is one thing your friends will tell you they don't want to know about your body?

DAY 234

List of things that I enjoy so much

DAY 235

List of things that you want to give away

DAY 236

Would you rather be on the moon than floating alone in the sky?

DAY 237

Would you rather have two options or one? Why?

DAY 238

Would you rather have a hot dog or fries that are greasy and full of fat?

DAY 239

What would you do differently if you could go back in time and do it all over?

DAY 240

What are the top five things that people say about you?

DAY 241

What is this one thing that gives me the ability to be this good?

DAY 242

What would you do if you were the teacher and everyone forgot his homework?

DAY 243

What are you grateful for that you're not doing for yourself?

What does your son need the most?

What is the best way to get along with someone who doesn't seem to accept you?

How do you become wealthy and healthy at the same time?

DAY 247

How would you describe the feeling when your voice is taken away?

DAY 248

How would you describe the feeling of being unlike humans?

DAY 249

Why did you decide to do the work you are doing now?

What's something you need to admit to yourself right now?

What does "there are two sides to every coin" mean to you?

What is the thing that makes you laugh the most?

DAY 253

What are your future plans and goals?

DAY 254

Do you have a favorite television show? Which character from the show would you be and why?

DAY 255

What website do you visit most often?

DAY 256

List of things that will happen when you go to sleep

DAY 257

Name one thing you're not

DAY 258

What would you do if the world stopped turning?

DAY 259

How is it that your thought processes are so limited that you only recognize changes in your heart when you see the signs that they're present?

DAY 260

If you're a man, what's the best quality of a woman?

DAY 261

How are you currently managing your time?

DAY 262

How do you measure your progress in life?

DAY 263

Do you prefer working alone or in small groups?

DAY 264

List of things that I would need to do in less than an hour

DAY 265

Do you ever feel like you're in a situation where you can't escape? Why?

DAY 266

If you had to choose one thing that made a better relationship, what would it be?

DAY 267

What's your favorite day of the year?

DAY 268

How do we determine what makes us happy at the moment?

DAY 269

Have you ever forgotten something very important? Tell about your experience.

DAY 270

If you could be in anyone's shoes, what would you tell them?

DAY 271

Which living person do you most despise?

DAY 272

What is the one thing that you were most relieved to discover?

DAY 273

How would you describe the feeling of being exposed?

DAY 274

List of things that will be rejected

DAY 275

Tell about an experience that prepared you to help someone in a challenging situation.

DAY 276

What would you say to someone who wants to feel important but is being weird and awkward?

DAY 277

How are you expected to care for your parents?

DAY 278

List of things that might occur

DAY 279

*Tell me about a time when you felt really happy and about a
time when you made someone else feel happy.*

DAY 280

Would you rather be loved or lost?

DAY 281

What situation has caused you to confront your ethics recently?

DAY 282

What trait did you admire in a relative, friend, classmate, or co-worker today?

DAY 283

If you were the owner of a horse, what type of horse would you choose to be?

DAY 284

What did you do today that made you laugh and feel happy?

DAY 285

What are your favorite television series with the worst endings?

DAY 286

What is most important to you to do?

DAY 287

What would be something you would do to relax?

DAY 288

If you could only have one book for the rest of your life, what would it be and why?

DAY 289

List of things that you wanted

DAY 290

What's going on in your head now?

DAY 291

Do you like to play the piano? Why?

What is a part of you that gets lost and forgotten?

What do you want in a romantic partner?

If you could change one thing in your life, what would it be?

What good thing has happened to you?

Would you rather be nothing or something?

What is one thing you have in common with everyone else?

DAY 298

What is the most annoying habit that other people have?

DAY 299

If you had to do nothing but work for a year, what would you do? Why?

DAY 300

What are your 10 most difficult moments to remember?

DAY 301

Say something about your background that helps people better understand you.

DAY 302

What is your favorite past time?

DAY 303

Would you ever take something someone else left behind?

DAY 304

What's your favorite way to take out a fire?

DAY 305

What did you like most about your first experience?

DAY 306

What do you wish you knew earlier?

When it might hurt their feelings, how do you feel about telling your friends the truth?

When you do stop drinking coffee/tea/soda?

If you had to select a group of people in the world today, would you prefer to be seen by someone famous or infamous, and why?

DAY 310

If you could have a day in which you were happy, what would you like it to be?

DAY 311

What is most important to you to be that voice in someone's life?

DAY 312

List of things that make you break down

DAY 313

Where would you travel, if you could go anywhere?

DAY 314

Do you have any bad habits? What are those?

DAY 315

What is more important to you, to be the biggest or to be the best?

DAY 316

If a genie granted you 3 wishes right now, what would you wish for?

DAY 317

Can you share something that has changed your life?

DAY 318

What is the one thing you want to have in your life?

DAY 319

Do you like working on one task at a time or should you be working on multiple things at the same time?

DAY 320

Would you rather be loved by everyone?

DAY 321

How am I qualified to be here?

DAY 322

What exactly are you waiting for?

DAY 323

If you could have one thing you could give to someone, what would it be?

DAY 324

You found a time machine that took you back 600 years. All you have are the clothes on your back. How do you tell the people that you're from the future?

DAY 325

What does it take to make someone else laugh?

DAY 326

What is one skill you wish you had and how would that make your life different?

DAY 327

What are some of the things that have been most interesting to you lately?

DAY 328

Do you have a fear of getting married? Why?

DAY 329

How do you deal with your own emotions?

DAY 330

If you were given unlimited and unassailable power, what would you do with that power? Would you use it to help others, or would you use it to hurt them?

DAY 331

List of things that would be easy to do on my own

DAY 332

If you could have any animal on Earth, what would it be?

DAY 333

How would you describe the feeling of being inside of a body for the first time?

DAY 334

Say something about your life that can be considered funny.

DAY 335

What was your favorite moment in elementary school and what did you remember?

DAY 336

Do you ever do things on the side to help yourself? Why?

DAY 337

What would you ask for if you could ask for anything in the universe and receive anything in return?

DAY 338

What are you going to do about it?

DAY 339

What is the most romantic thing you have done so far this year?

DAY 340

What is one thing you have in common with your colleagues?

DAY 341

What would you say is your greatest worry?

DAY 342

Who were the last two people you kissed?

What's the one thing that could actually change a young person's life?

What was it that you were waiting for?

Was there anything you missed? What was it?

What was the last thing you bought that you thought was a
lifesaver?

If you could do anything to get better at anything, what would
it be?

Has there ever been any negative feedback from other people in
your life?

DAY 349

What is the one thing which you must never do?

DAY 350

When you are angry, how do you look?

DAY 351

What is your most treasured memory?

DAY 352

What is one thing you have in common with your granddaughter?

DAY 353

What amazing thing did you do that no one was around to see?

DAY 354

If you could change your name to any other name, what would it be and why?

DAY 355

Have you been asked about your looks at work?

DAY 356

What was your biggest disappointment and how did you deal with it?

DAY 357

What is most important to you to be able to reveal your feelings about people and to be able to handle relationships?

DAY 358

Why would you want to change the world?

DAY 359

What is one thing about yourself you'd like to change?

DAY 360

Would you rather have one million dollars and be dead or one million dollars and be in hell?

DAY 361

What does your son/daughter do when they're scared?

DAY 362

What occupation do you think would be fascinating?

DAY 363

What is the one thing that every man should have in life?

DAY 364

What is one thing that you hope to accomplish this year that you haven't already done?

DAY 365

Think about your last breakup. What song do you think should have been playing at that moment?

DAY 366

What do you wish you had more of in life?